A Walk to the Spring House

A Walk to the Spring House

Poems

Sue Weaver Dunlap

Iris Press
Oak Ridge, Tennessee

Cover Photo: Raymond M. Dunlap

Book Design: Robert B. Cumming, Jr.

Iris Press
www.irisbooks.com

Library of Congress Cataloging-in-Publication Data

Names: Dunlap, Sue Weaver, 1953- author.
Title: A walk to the spring house : poems / Sue Weaver Dunlap.
Description: Oak Ridge, Tennessee : Iris Press, [2021] | Summary: "The
    poems in A Walk to the Spring House capture memories and relics of the
    poet's repository of experiences in the Southern Appalachian Mountains.
    These old mountains and her landscape shape the sections of the book,
    mountains that ultimately 'brace' and 'root' the poet who celebrates
    that she 'come[s]' from old. Not only does the poet 'pause to praise /
    the storytellers' and lay claim to her 'rooted inheritance,' she also
    pays homage to her own 'call to love.' The poet's landscape dwells deep
    in the water, the mines, the mountain farm, the family, the mill town,
    the hollers, the ancestors - Appalachian humankind and geography - its
    unique voice and place. These poems stitch together love, hurt, history,
    beliefs, and landscape, an amazing quilt where '[she] whisper[s] the old
    sweet of piney roses by the door.'"— Provided by publisher.
Identifiers: LCCN 2021030828 (print) | LCCN 2021030829 (ebook) | ISBN
    9781604542585 (paperback) | ISBN 9781604548174 (ebook)
Subjects: LCGFT: Poetry.
Classification: LCC PS3604.U5524 W35 2021 (print) | LCC PS3604.U5524
    (ebook) | DDC 811/.6—dc23
LC record available at https://lccn.loc.gov/2021030828
LC ebook record available at https://lccn.loc.gov/2021030829

Acknowledgments

Grateful acknowledgment is made to the editors of the following journals and anthologies in which the poems listed were published for the first time, sometimes in a slightly different form.

Anthology of Appalachian Writers, Vol. V: "Harvest," "Spirit Place"
Bloodroot, 2018: "Fairy Rose Bilderback"
Kakalak 2019: "Place Names," "Steeping Home"
Pine Mountain Sand & Gravel, Vol. 21: Appalachia Acting Up: "Practiced Hand"
Pine Mountain Sand & Gravel, Vol. 22: Appalachian (Un)Broken: "Chota"

In Memory of My Sister/Cousin, Robin Nicholson Craig

"We whisper the old sweet of piney roses by the door."

•   •   •

Storytelling and family, lines of memory and poems of heart have shaped this collection. I hold in my heart the plethora of people who have inspired my poet's voice and nurtured my writing space. I am indebted to my many teachers and workshop friends who have shored up my confidence and critiqued my work over the years. God and faith have guided me to special people in this journey of writing: The amazing poets in Chapbook classes led by the awesome poet and friend Connie Green, my Table Rock Writers' friends led by the talented Georgann Eubanks, and my poet sisters Dee Stribling, Kim Blum-Hyclak, and Laurie Wilcox-Meyer nurtured by our ties that bind hearts and words. Darnell Arnoult brought me from the abstract to the concrete and has loved me like a sister, and Joseph Bathanti mentored and loved with his beautiful spirit. The mountains and hollers of the Appalachian Mountains rooted me and brought me to the altar of kith and kin to celebrate and preserve our stories. My heart thrives here. I am humbled by the many editors who have considered my work and published my poems. I am also humbled by Bob and Beto Cumming for giving this collection a home at their beautiful press. My kin travel with me across time and space in my poetry—what a gift! I cherish the students I carry in my heart every day. And to my husband Raymond—you have been my tree of support on this journey, keeping the home fires burning so I can pursue my words and dreams. I dedicate this book to my closest kin, Cousin Robin—our paths of memory are twined in our mountains we call home.

There is something beautiful about all scars of whatever nature.
A scar means the hurt is over, the wound is closed and healed, done with.

—Harry Crews

Contents

Ink • 11

BRACE ME, ROOT ME

Soul Praise • 15
Traveling to Tumbling Creek • 16
Place Names • 17
Gathering Home • 18
Chota • 19
Finding Uncle Buddy Goode: Upon Entering His King James Bible • 20
Cotton Evil • 22
Marigold Dream • 23
Leslie Street Peddler • 24
Annie Goode Weaver • 25
Papaw Ray's Cub • 26
Fairy Rose Bilderback • 27
Morning • 28
I Love • 29
Holler Cousins • 30
April's Breath • 31
Miracle in If Only • 32
Crystal Savior • 33

GIRD ME, MARK ME

Never Child • 37
Dawn Denied • 38
Mother and Daughter • 39
Rusty Promise • 40
Mid-July Morning • 41
Robin's Ridge • 42
Altar of Kith and Kin • 43
Twilight Feeding • 44
Ice Cream Truck Melody • 45
Shutters • 46
Moved On • 47
Shelter Family • 48

My Brother's Knife • 49

The Yellow Dress • 51

Ruminate • 53

July Heat • 54

Ode to My Shin Scar • 55

Grow Me, Warm Me

In the Beginning • 59

Frost • 60

Video Memory • 61

Prayer Stations • 62

Snow Light • 63

Practiced Hand • 64

Blue Ridge Dying • 66

Knoxville Girl • 67

Front Yard Hideaway • 68

Harvest • 69

Cane Break on Highway 68 • 70

Soothe Me, Promise Me

Smoky Visit • 73

Night Walk to Our Spring House • 74

Mast of Plenty • 75

Summer Storm • 76

Triangle • 77

Soul Sad • 78

Upon the Evening of His Passing • 79

Spring Confusion • 80

Today • 81

Narrow Slit • 82

Steeping Home • 83

Summer Passing • 84

Spirit Place • 85

Home • 86

Mountain Quiet • 87

Gray Blue Days • 88

Stitched Prayers • 89

Carry Me, Love Me

Heart Breath • 93
Act IV: House to Half • 94
A Call to Love • 95
Coffee-Stained Kitchen Talk • 96
June Hay Fields • 97
Love Lifted • 98
Papaw's Heart • 99
Our Season of Grieving • 100
Scattered Remains • 101
Whippoorwill Dream • 102
Front Porch Haiku • 103
Quilt Speak • 104
Rocking Chair Porch • 105
Dog Days • 106
Night of the Soul • 107
Appalachia Old • 108

Ink

Poetry rests in the air a few more minutes,
                waits to be fingered onto this yellow page.
                Scrambled words pause, ready
                        to be molded, sculpted
                                from lead in my pencil.

No form. No lines.

Images come first, tiptoe past scrambled words,
                seek to find their place on this clean-lined
                        paper. My mother's iambic pentameter
                                beats the poem from images to words
                                        to lines, like the journey

of memory from experience to heart to ink.

Brace Me, Root Me

Soul Praise

My soul lies in Sylco Cemetery, a dividing line between old
country and new ground, where in spring I pause to praise
Goode and Woods as I lie down, mingle my dirt with theirs.

My soul lies along Tumbling Creek, its path following mountains,
tumbling its way to the Ocoee River in early summer where
I pause, praise my Cherokee grandmother and her people.

My soul lies in Lula's Holler, now empty and lonely, the road
to our graves rutted and worn, where in dreaded heat of late
summer I pause to praise and embrace cicadas and dreams.

My soul lies along the trails of Big Frog Mountain in autumn
glory where I pause to praise my Mealer grandfather, follow
his paths and smell the swirling leaves and rotting bark.

My soul lies on Kimsey Highway, its twists and turns sharp
and deep where in winter's waning days I pause to praise
the storytellers and kneel at my own trail crossing.

Traveling to Tumbling Creek

They crossed the swelling of the Little Tennessee,
he an outlaw from family and country, she, his wife,
taken from splintered ground, where her red skin marked
her for life. They searched for home beyond the river.
With their two small boys they came to Tumbling Creek,
a narrow divide of hardship between the mountains,
from Snowbird in Eastern Carolina and small Georgia towns,
ancestors of mine, long forgotten before my conception
yet dwelling in the eddy of my mother's sac. I seek them
as I walk in fields of barren ground and fool's gold
in the low branch at Salina's door.

Place Names

from "A Bear Hunt in the Smokies,"
Our Southern Highlanders by Horace Kephart

Mountain men slide through place names, their bear dogs ready.
They rest at Siler's Meadow, slap cold water on stubbled faces
at Forney's Creek, camp at Rip Shin Thicket near Gunstick Laurel,
head out at day's first break, think to find meat at Clingman Dome.
They don't cross Sugarland Mountains, follow sign from Little River
near Thunderhead and Briar Knobb, track an old fellow around
Devil's Court House, Block House, and Wooly Ridge near Bear Pen.
Dogs take chase between Briar Knob and Laurel Top, end him near
Saddle-back. Two shots. His parts shared among highlander hunters.

Gathering Home

Dark comes down Grandma Goode's holler in early summer
like a tide rolls in on a full moon night. Woods dirt seeps onto her

one lane road, borders between honeysuckle sweet and fermented
leaves, a love - hate affair back dropped with the rising breathing

of cicadas that quilt us onto her porch. We twine ourselves
around her rocker. Older kin claim cane bottom chairs, lean back,

light a rolled Prince Albert cigarette. Cousins cover pine
slat floors, nestle closer as the mountain cat cries like lore

from the Knoxville Girl sung quiet, Poppy's fiddle sorrowful
mourns for her rosy cheeks and lips under her lover's knife.

Chota

Hear tell folks around here boiled dirt to leech salt,
back on Defeat Ridge, a time when a man's tools
held his family, a hand saw, open and light, handy
on the swing blade, hand scythe cutting a swathe
through burnt-red sage grass. Tater Branch back
home across the tracks. Folks not really gone, we
just can't see them right now like the year whites
moved Cherokee west, the year of no sun, the year
we survived, here in this last place of eternal fire.

Finding Uncle Buddy Goode:
Upon Entering His King James Bible

Uncle Buddy loved the prophets, especially Isaiah,
marked scripture in both the Old and New Testaments,
words to build his sermons. A lay preacher who cracked
his Bible to lead his flock, he oft turned to Ezekiel,
Ecclesiastes, and Proverbs for wisdom from his elders,
next to the Gospels, noted passages with his mark
guided by the words of Jesus in red. Never heard him
preach, this uncle, only the remembering of suit visits,
his Sunday hat a bit stained around the brim, like sins
he sought to lead his flock from come third Sunday
every month back at the Freewill Baptist Church
of Archville where now he slumbers on a hill facing heaven.

And he said, this lay preacher uncle of mine:

The words of the preacher, God now accepteth thy works,
in thy labor which thou takest under the sun. We will
remember thy love more than wine, for the reward of
his hands shall be given him, saith the Lord God of Hosts.

Let us pray, Amen. And Uncle Buddy's clean white
handkerchief came from his pocket with his right hand
while his left held an open Bible, its thin pages still
to the air in this small mountain church, old lady fans
an advertisement to a Polk County Funeral home,
the only movement save this preacher man's deliberate
march across Zion at the front of the church, his face
drawn red, his thread-worn suit shiny against his aged
brown hands, black shoes spit-shined to a high gloss.

And Ezekiel said, I will sprinkle clean water upon you,
I will give you a new spirit, I will be your God. And do
you sinners know the Lord, huh, thy God, huh, forever
burn in Hell, my brothers and sisters, huh, Amen.

And the preacher man loosed his tie and the demons
of these sinner folks loosed themselves as well to find
escape through the windows of July heat hell suffocation.

And let us pray, Amen.

*For the prophet, huh, Isaiah, huh, promised - the Lord
God Almighty will make thee an eternal excellency,
a joy of many generations, huh, and said, I the Lord
am the Redeemer, the mighty One of Jacob, huh,
and sinners, huh, the Lord will be glorified. And
so saith the scripture this day unto you.*

In this march across Zion at Freewill Baptist
the sinners one by one left their place and joined
the preacher man at the altar for one last call
of redemption. And let us pray, Amen.

*And if any one of you gathered here, sinners all,
huh, feels the flames of hell lap at your feet, huh,
throw down that ball of fire, let Jesus, huh, sweet
Jesus, huh, take that burden sinner, and we shall
go down to this River Jordan, huh, and wash you
clean, huh, oh sinner, don't let Satan burn today.*

And Brother Goode took off his suit coat, threw
it on the altar like he was casting out Satan
at Freewill Baptist Church. The walls swelled
with moans from sinners and saints, all hypnotized
by the preacher's words, his left hand outreached
Bible still draped open, his right hand stretched
to heaven, sweat a constant stream from his chin.

His voice whispered,

*let's go down to the River Jordan and wash
you clean, oh brothers and sisters. And the Lord
said, Amen.*

Cotton Evil

Uncle Jim and Aunt Sis couldn't field children along rows of cotton,
one or both of them barren on Sand Mountain. Alabama poor ground

dead to regret. Poppy's house grew pretty girls, a labor to feed
his family when mining copper died in his hands. Poppy pulled

two girls bathed in beauty from watered wood floors, sent them
to walk ground where earth shapes feet with no shoes. Cotton knows.

Blood trickles in the barn, stains white cotton.
And little girls cry for home.

Marigold Dream

Marigolds thrive best around garden's edge,
keep bugs away, at least that's what old wives
say. Grandma Lula tended a garden until 1956,
when Poppy's bad heart failed. An old black
and white photo holds proof Grandma knew dirt,
the hoe and how to use it. She felt the camera,
turned toward it, her face not quite smiling,
a bonnet to shield the sun's rays. Grandma Lula
of my childhood shunned garden plots and tools,
her food the labor of others. Grandma Lula didn't
dig dirt, plant or tend flowerbeds. We never planted
marigolds, just stopped to smell her snowball bush
creek side, laden white this early May morning.

Leslie Street Peddler

Grandmother Weaver thanked God no babies to support
from his pittance change at day's end. Papaw gone
all day door to door. His peddler's case overflowed
with snuff tins, both trouser- and apron-pocket sized,
needles, pins, spools of thread, black, white, and blue,
magnifying glasses, Earl Sloan's horse liniment
and Carter's liver pills, penny licorice or balls of twine,
maybe a rubber ball. Harvest time brought corn and beans,
potatoes and watermelons from his garden or Market Square
farmers. His borrowed wagon and horse carried his wares.

Annie Goode Weaver

My fingers trace each letter of her name,
paternal grandmother, this granite stone
sole link to a woman I never knew, a marker
in an overgrown cemetery. Annie Goode
came to Knoxville in 1900, a textile worker
looking for a job. She bought twelve plots
in a church cemetery on Keith Street, found
a tinker husband. Today, I read aloud her name
in a 1934 Knoxville City Directory, its thin paper
aged and fine, printed after she died, casualty
of a broken neck when she tripped, fell down
steep steps and sprawled out onto Leslie Street.

Papaw Ray's Cub

His Papaw Ray bought the shiny red Farmall Cub tractor in 1953,
had it delivered. The two of them stood under a middle-aged oak.
The four-year-old grandson mimicked his Papaw, folded arms
across his tiny chest. They circled this magnificent beauty, tried
to contain their excitement. His papaw took the first ride, learned
the steering and the clutch, nuances of a new machine ready to serve.
The spirited boy bounced around from side to side, ready to begin
his love affair with red tractors. Even after the axle crushed his young
foot, skin and bones mixed in blood in his high-topped brown leather
boots, weeks, months of surgery, grafts, and needles, the little boy
carried his love strong, conquered the Farmall Cub and other machines,
green, orange, more red, and white, until that day his Papaw left,
and the cub with their history became his, now laid out in parts
on tables, a restoration of life for a little boy and his 1953 Farmall Cub.

Fairy Rose Bilderback

Grass dried brittle in Fairview Baptist Church Cemetery.
Dusty road dirt swirled as we wound our way to the top.
Blue signs nailed to trees promised our arrival, numbered
miles not given. Fairy Rose Bilderback breathed for a day
in 1941, a promised bud of love to frolic. Crisp-veined
autumn leaves crunched the path where Fairy Rose held
dominion over all the babies rowed up around her. Do
they pretend full-bodied lives when stars dance each night
or notice the newcomers' numbers dwindle at their feet?

Morning

Air lies still
>> sweet in the holler
>>> after late night rains.

Crimson cardinals shrill
>> their hungry arrival
>>> at gorged feeders.

Bears search ample
>> woods and yard-sweet
>>> acorns and hickory nuts.

Turkeys leave late
>> treetop roosts, roust
>>> spirits from slumber.

We wake slow
>> hidden behind bolted
>>> doors, spooning minutes.

I weary wear
>> bone stiff years,
>>> grief sad alone.

I Love

sunsets high on Clingman's Dome, solid moon rising,
juxtaposition of time and space, flowers that appear
unbidden in early April, purple phlox and bloodroot
woods' growth, ivy, her roots grabbing ground on limestone
boulders jutting above our spring cave, gradations of red,
orange, and yellow—maples, dogwoods, oaks shift from fall
into cold, tangled covers, new love wrapped like a canopy
of foreverness, toes and fingers curled, naked mortality,
unexpected opaque familiarity of blue-veined hands, cemented.

Holler Cousins

They lived in a shotgun house at the end of a dirt road
glistening with fool's gold, pyrite flecks against black woods.
Mountain laurel thick along the shallow creek mixed with memory
wakes my dreams. Throaty laughter rolled down the ridge with every
visit I made to these mountain cousins. The front room of the house
sat at the back, the path to its door blocked by stacked firewood
and the wash table, a fresh bucket of water near the shallow dented
wash basin. A tired towel drooped from a rusty nail. Two iron beds
stayed off limits to our play lest Grandma catch us singing, dancing,
jumping. A worn sofa and straight back cane chairs pulled close
to a weary hearth. The kitchen welcomed at the front of the house,
a long oak table sheltered with faded oil cloth, the core. We watched
the cooking, heard our family memory, nodded off near the warm
cook stove. Cornbread browned its way to supper. Play days ended
in the middle room, whispered grownups distant, our snuggle bed born.

Its sag pulled cousins to me.
Its center wrapped us.

April's Breath

She sought to wake me subtle, a nudge against winter remnants,
bleak rain, light too short, dark cut my cadence. Purple phlox
lined the windy drive like soldiers greet wounded fresh from battle.
March frogs orchestrated praise hymns from the barn bog, escorted
me up the weary steps. I first noticed late light when bats dove
near my head scavenging for supper gnats. I paused, ready to shed
my soaked coat at the door. Whippoorwills and blackberry white
walked in together while trillium teased and may apples blanketed
our holler. But it was the lady slippers, their bulging bellies
the backdrop for courting dances of my three toms with puffed
chests and draped brown capes that wrapped me.

Miracle in If Only

I yearn to hear my dead voices again.
    Silence fills a lonesome world
        created by this void.

They come from light. Who could predict
    these faithful kinfolk would disappear,
        slide into darkness?

Her passing over without me by her side
    started this onslaught of quiet
        in my head, my heart.

Is she holding them all somewhere,
    captured them as they arranged
        her homecoming?

Come back to me. What miracles
    lie in the if onlys? I didn't
        help her over.

She shunned my faithful attendance.
    If only I had been there, I could
        have held them all.

Crystal Savior

Redemption came to a five-year-old girl at the top of the sky,
stair steps to heaven, Mama described dimensioned rays of sun
drawn against the sky. When Jesus beckoned me from His throne
near the highest point, I did not tarry in my backyard sanctuary.
I raced up crystal stairs resolved to meet Him, sit on His lap, eager,
attentive. He whispered, never forget me, young girl, life couched
early in thorns. He held rosemary and lilac, scent to bathe my pain.

Gird Me, Mark Me

Never Child

A child's spirit never landed in me—
     not at conception
     not at birth
     never.
I sensed no warm blanket to comfort or grow me.

In this sixth decade of my life, I think of the wood bore.
It hovers around soft wood, finds the smallest nick
     and drills, drills until it finds center.

I couldn't find any slit in the steel armor, a melded
     cocoon purposed to shield the little girl me.

No place to indwell—

                    Jump rope
                    Dolls
                    Tag
                    Ball
                    Hide and seek

playful child me,
bore into my core
wrap me in laughing giggles,
run without fear.

The child I was never grew.
Water doesn't penetrate steel.

Dawn Denied

Mornings after Daddy's beer and whiskey ground, he denies
the cotton-mouthed hangover, seeks cures in black coffee
and Camel cigarettes, dawn reduced to tools and blue Chevy truck.

Mornings after Daddy's beer and whiskey ground, Mama pulls
herself to kitchen chores, biscuits and sausage, eggs and gravy,
rues his coffee mess, slips on her red apron, tight under heavy breasts.

Mornings after Daddy's beer and whiskey ground, ten-year-old me
vows to hide away, fractured sleep, waits until the front door slams,
steals into my mother's space, dawn not quite breaking through.

Mother and Daughter

First grade terrors began at the solid oak paneled door, my stubby hand
white-knuckle glued to Mama's work-hewn one. She led me to the door,

separation new and raw for us, six years this mother-daughter journey.
I resisted small green enamel chairs circling a round wooden table low

to the floor. Dark heavy casings framed leaded glass windows, my light
for daydreams beyond alphabet letters standing tall in stiff salute around

these classroom walls. The terrarium with emerald moss, rocks, twigs
held my attention more than eight stubby crayolas of blue, orange, red

in their box bed. Lustre waxed floors squeaked our comings and goings.
A scary hall led to beef stew lunches, library books, principal's office.

And I cried every day until the light faded.

Rusty Promise

Not once did Mama promise it would be easy, this notion
of her early leaving, a life like a wrought iron fence, rusty
veiled in hard hope, cold metal forged in beauty and necessity.

Each of us knew the rock of her chair began too soon for me
to keep her. Reasonable women have babies in their youth,
not when the change mars their wholeness. A baby pushed

her forties into swirling rapids over jutting rocks, cut
her feet when she tried to climb out of deep rage. Chained
tight. Mama faded before escape, anointed in early leaving.

Mid-July Morning

Sunbeam white bread, JFG peanut butter,
the creamy kind, homemade blackberry jelly,
seedless, Cut-rite waxed paper wrapped,
grape Kool-aid in a Mason pint jar, no cookie,
brown paper sack, chores done, little girl set free.

Don't come home till suppertime.

Nancy Drew mystery, three cedar trees, clean
swept ground, hidden hideaway, shut out world.
Hard hurt hides secrets, cross-legged dreamer,
made-up stories, secrets safe, little girl breathe gentle.

Don't come home till suppertime.

Robin's Ridge

Her mountain gardens paled long before first frost found its way
to Robin's Ridge. Roses faded, petals fell fast, her pruning shears
abandoned on her front porch shelf. Morning conversations
with zinnias, marigolds, and daisies only memory when her legs
failed to find solid comfort on warm ground. Finches and cardinals
flew away in sorrow, feeders left to hated cowbirds, their thievery
ignored. No strength to push them away. Bob-tailed Jinx and three-legged
Miss Moses fattened all summer, sought her out for naps on warm boards
when her rocking chair became her strength, quiet space alone. Hopeless
cold settled in when the last of her fell away with gray curls all gone.
Nakedness resides beneath a mask of radiant poison waiting on time to go.

Altar of Kith and Kin

I bring the faded flower tablecloth to our table once a year.
In quiet homage to kith and kin, I unfold this sixty-year-old
past, grip the long side, raise my arms in praise, cover our
oak table. I caress the daisies along its border, curse cigarette
holes sprinkled across its girth. I sit, close my eyes, smell
lukewarm coffee tinged with milk in heavy white cups Mama
and Daddy used in their restaurant of youth. I dream up details
about that time in their past before I came to them. Sunday
dinner over, kith and kin linger at this altar of family, play
Scrabble, keen wordsmiths across and down, lies and truths.

Twilight Feeding

I watched you feed your mother this evening.
Darkness seeped into the room like her shallow
pool of breaths heralded an unwanted visitor,
one she has kept on the other side of living,
unwilling to cross the divide to peace and rest.

You were careful to cut each bite of pumpkin
pie, crust unwanted, almost dangerous to her
unwilling throat that strangles with each try
at sustenance to prolong her staying. I imagined
you sitting in a high chair, your mother unsteady

with feeding until she found her way as a young
mother, not quite beyond childhood dolls
and high school dances. Tonight, in this intimate
moment not planned or wanted, the natural twist
of life's path puts you both in the twilight of leaving.

Ice Cream Truck Melody

I remember special treats from the ice cream truck, its sing-song
melodies repeating each summer afternoon. A clan of youngsters
wore out the trees, front yard ball field, and grapevine swings
in deep woods all morning until lunch time. Our larder offered
up fried potato sandwiches on white bread slathered in JFG
mayonnaise, our drink the flavor of the day Kool-Aid.

Early afternoon found us down at the creek, some of us sitting
on the bridge dangling bare feet over those chasing crawdads
and trying out new slingshots on snake feeders. We learned
the art of listening and telling stories, knew the tricksters.
Each of us careful not to drop our quarter for frozen treats,
we circled the truck like dragonflies on the eddy. I sit alone

in the kitchen of a woman who lingers between here and there,
a house empty except for her treasures. In the distance, I hear
the echo of an ice cream truck tune, recall my childhood treats.
My husband offers a frozen bar. Today, two dollars for ice cream
on a stick, memory wrapped warm. We sit quiet in her house, silent.

Shutters

She can't open the shutter.
No one on the other side hears her
ask first one then another to take
her home, her body or mind
not willing to do it herself.
Why should the gloaming
of eighty-four years be
different, this day of death
when she can't cross some
great chasm that divides
life and death. The dying
swirl in the dark. We wait,
count breaths until dawn.

Moved On

We live in stone.
The newcomers
created new place
where others stood.
Lived, died old,
moved not gone
wait alone, still.

Shelter Family

His father once told me:
     You are not a family,
     his son and I,
     no babies flowed.

I balked in anger at his drunk
spat words, cradled the hurt
of no formed babies, vowed
to stand firm on our family
rock, his son and I.

No nursery occupied
save the line of dogs and cats,
our shelter family.

In these years of children
and grandchildren withered
on their vines, I parse
what ifs, wonder
what friends and family
see now in the gnarled
fingers of life's end.

Alone we stand, he and I,
no close kin
to abide our pain,
brush our tears.

My Brother's Knife

Rainy days
    ache my shin scar
        like objects of you
            cry in my heart of loss.

Your hunting
    knife slept in brown
        and tan leather sheath,
            blade sharp and glistening.

Hours you spent
    with a whet rock
        and spit, razor sharp
            ready for practice throws

at our aged
    mimosa tree,
        a bull's eye center
            mark aligned for your height,

precise throw.
    That knife in my
        hand, forbidden game
            in our childhood Eden.

Alone, I
    stood posed, ready.
        Aim. Palm against cold,
            breathed fear, excitement.

Now, released
    measured against
        my height, no bull's eye,
            only a thud, misfire

steel tip bone deep.
My blood gushed
like miserable tears
flowing the night you left.

The Yellow Dress

—S & W Cafeteria:
Knoxville, Tennessee,
Spring 1967

Eighth grade banquet, our teacher said.
Everyone shall go, she said.

We will make a new dress, my mother said.
No, I will not go, I said.

Everyone will have store-bought dresses.
I shall not go, I said.

We will go to Lerner's Department Store, she said.
Buy you a dress, she said.

We will ride the bus to Gay Street, she said.
Make a day of it.

Try the yellow one, she said.
A line, a pleat in the front, white collar.

We will buy white shoes, a white bag, she said.
I will look hideous, I said. Yellow will not work.

The other girls have more stylish mothers, I thought.
You will be beautiful, she said, yellow dress in hand.

Across the way is the S & W, she said.
Your dad will drop you. You will have fun, she said.

Dad drove his pick-up in silence.
I sat in my hideous self, looked straight ahead.

I will not have fun, I did not say.
You will have fun, he did not say.

I cannot eat chicken in public, I said.
Bobby Shoun ate chicken with his fingers.

He was taller than all of us, posed with girls
for memory pictures, laughed through our pain.

You will have fun, they said,
to the girl in the hideous yellow dress.

Ruminate

I remember Mama's busy hands,
her needle purposeful and steady.
I understand in this breaking day
the lonely life of the woman set
aside, the good all used and worn.

In the hour between sleepless
night and watchful dawn,
I sit in the shadow, parse
the here, ruminate my past,
deny the tomorrow.

July Heat

I gathered red-scarred hills
and gully memories
on a suffering searing Saturday
in July when our older kin
led us on a lark over red-burnt
ground, copper glistening
against our bare feet,
all of us ill-prepared to scoot
down, keen-edged rocks
and burrs assaulting bare skin.
I dared not falter or complain
lest I be scorned by mocking
tongues. Their power prevailed,
propelled me into pain.
Sweat slid into my eyes,
burned like the nettles
blistering my feet.
And I ran until I stopped.

Ode to My Shin Scar

Scar—
>whiter than skin tone,
>hidden tight,
>pain still healing
>like my heart,
>bigger than mimosa pinks,
>smaller than oak trees,
>bone deep and tired.

Grow Me, Warm Me

In the Beginning

I sought aloneness,
an early morning call
to life. My hands
cupped dew-drenched
grass, nectar to wash
my night-dream face.

I sought quiet
from mockingbird
chatter. Sweet sounds
muted morning chores
behind splintered planked
oak-washed walls.

I sought dreams,
followed chimney smoke,
its path trailed light
down Yellow Lead Branch,
fool's gold promises
shiny below clear water.

I sought purpose.
My heart loved
beyond red hills.
Copper and Sulphur
choked my desires
dulled by hell.

I sought truth,
my womanhood
lonely for dreams,
needs and wants,
dayshine and nightshine
lost in lonely.

Frost

Frost-glistened tips of grass blades at dawn's first light catch me, pull
me into cold air, a place to walk the wild puppy, her nose fast in search
of leftover scents, a buck's trail still fresh across the wet weather branch,
clear and fast, her playground for running and jumping, ice water rolling
along her black back, webbed feet at home. We greet this day, when quiet
begats peace and frost promises breath trails like vapor jets crisscrossing
blue skies, like words and lines finding form, impressions on winter ground.

Video Memory:
Upon Finding Dad on the Internet

Daddy died in 1992 yet tonight his face visits my small screen,
a technology he never knew, his time long before the young
videographer came to ask him scripted questions, answers
no one expected. Daddy the rebel rouser, a storied man
whose name wore the black mark from 1934, stranded
without a job because he walked a picket line. His story
fermented until young academia recorded his aged blue
eyes mocking their naiveté. Tonight, Daddy stared out
at me, handsome in turquoise, his arms still tanned, toned.
His hands curved around my heart, captured my dreams.

Prayer Stations

Elders of the church built this statue garden,
wrote prayers for recitation, grew me taller,
my hand raised heavenward to keep watch
over stones of sorrow under these old pin oaks,
said the chipped white statue.

I wonder what it is like to grow beyond birth,
touch the face of Mama not the face of God,
said baby Fairy Rose.

Cemetery after cemetery we visit along dusty windy
mountain roads. I, too, walk among the remembered,
said the red-headed golden.

Snow Light

Aunt Leona lived one ridge over from us
here in Cold Springs, last kin with an outdoor
toilet. The spring before she died, she asked
for a floodlight for her yard. Sick with
her breast illness chewing from the inside
out, her garden grew fallow, her bed weary.
Turkeys companioned her days, lingered, ate
slow, gave her a show. Nights begged beauty.
Snow swirled around the light, its gentle path
her ease. Tonight, snow arrived late in our
holler. I sit in the back room and watch.
White swirls around my light.

Practiced Hand

1

Daddy said our names mean something,
stand honest and true, don't disgrace.
He quit school to work
in Brookside Cotton Mill,
young, really. His name
took the black mark.
Striker. Rebel.

2

The Great Depression let its own way out, urged
on by public works and the war. Daddy walked
his way to the army recruiter station, wanted
to sign his name, ready to serve. Army
said no. Too old. Kids at home need
a dad. He walked back, tried again.

3

The 1950s brought a measure of good fortune, his own
boss now. Daddy held his fountain pen tight, formed
cursive letters of his name, practiced over and over
until his "W" mimicked the perfect model. Sister
practiced Daddy's name until she forged
his checks. Bank called. Holy wrath fell.

4

Frailty came, took Daddy, his signature the first
    casualty, subtle at first, a little shaky along the straight
        lines leading into the curves, then more aggressive
            in its consumption when the curly "q's" dropped
                from his "W." I began to sign for him here
                and there, banks and hospitals.
Mourned.

Blue Ridge Dying

A sixty-year-old farmer named B. H. Sebolt eyed his
Blue Ridge Mountain garden then looked toward
Ducktown Basin across the Tennessee line
near the badlands of copper smelters.

His drawn up peas, potatoes, cabbage,
and corn victimized, a wasteland
of human cruelty in this hellhole
blister, its red-ravaged hills

and gullies home to miners
and families along open
heaps of roasting
sulfur edged

by sedge grass
and cat briar

until the mountains slid to their death.

Knoxville Girl

I heard an old blue grass ballad on the radio today. Home
caught my breath, sorrowful banjo and harmonica blended
in harmony, the Knoxville Girl taking a walk down by the river
with a lover, bittersweet ballad from the old country. This young
girl died by the hand of her handsome man and his knife. Mama sang
for me this song she learned at her family's knee, tragedy across the ocean
long ago. This tune and my mother playing the banjo by ear, soul sad.
I wove my own story about a dark-haired, blue-eyed girl along
the Tennessee River a few miles from home. I sang Mama's
tragedy, my own rewrite of her story tucked in fingers
finding memory along banjo strings. Her young
lover John Talley dead, his baby on the way.

Front Yard Hideaway

Thick-trunked sweet-blossomed mimosa trees
anchor my nine-year-old self, mark bases
in a game of front yard ball, our hands
firm against smooth tree skin mark
us safe. At last bean-picking, the second
base mimosa tree shades the back of Daddy's
blue Chevy pick-up truck, its bed rounded
with bean vines, the mound speckled
with white half-runners and yellow wilted
leaves, the tail gate a resting place, his long
legs dangling, sure hands pulling beans
to us, family gathered nearby, our web-woven
lawn chairs tight circled, each one of us
tasked to string and break, prepare for cans.
In heart black times, these trees shelter
this broken child. I sit on a wide-berthed
plank wedged tight in the highest fork.
My body hides, looks out a pink-framed
window. Imagined voices soothe, caress
away all casualties of hurt and love.

Harvest

I once heard that Watson Gregory still plowed
using his old mule Blue over at Oak Grove.
Bet his hands knew callouses and pain.

Poppy Goode plowed with his old mule
down on Brush Creek. Never knew that mule's
name. Poppy died long before I thought to ask.

My daddy and mama turned their garden
by hand after the neighbor plowed with his
old Massey tractor. Creek bottom grew

with ease. Mama let fertilizer drift
through her fingers, one handful at a time
while I walked behind dragging a trace chain

to mix dirt and fertilize. I dropped
pink-colored corn six inches apart. Daddy
followed me. His hoe pulled a silky cover,

loose to let germinating happen fast.
We worked, the three of us at this first
planting of beans, corn, field and sweet,

enough of both to feed all their offspring
and more, once hard times set in again
as often happened after the labor of harvest.

Cane Break on Highway 68

All night, this soft rain from the distant past.
No wonder I sometimes waken as a child.
—Ted Kooser

The cane break smothers their breakfast pull-off on Highway 68,
now a squatters' camp tucked along Coker Creek. Mama and Daddy
greet dawn over an open fire, coffee brewed first, the coffee pot
dented and pitted, then a breakfast of bacon and eggs. Light bread
sops the greasy egg plates clean. Random mornings they make
this sojourn until my grandmother dies in 1978 and reasons to travel
beyond the mountain to the Basin die with her, like their morning fire.

Soothe Me, Promise Me

Smoky Visit

I smell his Camel cigarettes first. Smoke passes over my bed
like it did when we visited Grandma Goode's house. He would
have his first one of the morning, me snuggled under layers
of cover where I waited for him to finish. I play possum.
Cold and warm and Camels build a thin cocoon.

I hear his cough before I feel him in the room. His hack held
his history from textile mills to our coal stoker furnace and all
the jobs between. Daddy sits beside me in a cane bottom
chair Grandpa Goode made, its small frame not quite
accommodating to six foot five Daddy.

He slides down to the "tenth joint of his backbone," long
legs stretched out before him like felled trees, waiting. I
breathe easy, wait for him to speak, some sign I'm not
crazy. A dead man's visit. Daddy looks around the room,
takes in the finish work, slips away into morning.

Night Walk to Our Spring House

I gathered courage and candle, my purpose to fetch
sweet milk, dim end of day melted away, flickering
fireflies just out, shadows of tree limbs against
orange gloaming of sunset west. At spring's edge
salamanders skidded into a chilled late summer

spring, the flare of my light ebbing and flowing,
floor stone slick with beaded sheen of sweet water.
Inside the stacked stone house, troughed nectar
guised in white luxury held my aim steady, strong,
the gutterswell dark. Up the path at the house,

Mommy's fried cabbage and cornbread waited me,
purple beets glistened in a white porcelain bowl
alongside pole beans and new potatoes rendered
with salt bacon, sweet memories of home on my
tongue, corn fresh from the cob, food to fill our

red oak table, center me within these walls,
and as I turn with milk in hand, Grandmother
touches my elbow, whispers stand tall, use all
gifts placed in your hands. I leave the springhouse.
The moon now lightens my way back to a home

of bounty on shelves of toil and gratitude,
Grandmother's fingers long since journeyed away.
Memories raised like Braille read like words in my
book where spring's flow persists in memory,
marking my way, encouragement to unearth
gratitude this day when love springs.

Mast of Plenty

I linger in bed this early November morning, root in deep
under layers of covers, embrace the cool of the hour, wait
for light to find mountain tops, honor the full-throated giggles
of my sister poets. We search meaning along this path we meander,
praise the living with words and hopes, lines and love. Stanzas
speak our heart love this day in God's valley of peace.

Summer Storm

I missed Mama something fierce this summer. Unleashed clichéd pundits of wisdom would have been welcome, even sought after. I saw her knowing eyes everywhere I turned, sensed her mischief making in my life, heard deep laughter in my kitchen when I grabbed flour from the freezer to make cornbread, a cake-like disaster. I felt her touch my cheek with warm early morning winds. Summer storms rolled up our holler before twilight took hold, thunder and lightning one continual loop of magic. Sheets of rain washed late dog days in a muddy rush down the creek. Tonight, trees stand silent, the pause between day and night. Cardinals complain when supper hour ends, their desire to pick at seeds battles the call to roost. And to the East, three evening stars sparkle their shimmering edges until dark takes the day.

Triangle

Our hearts can't find their paths to death.
Tough will and living hard cut deep.
Food leaves the mouth, water comes
in trickles. They all look alike, brothers
and sisters of mine, dying. No uniqueness
in their death masks. Daddy looks at me
from their eyes, long fingers, wide palms,
wasted. We reside in this triangle, wait
until the last breath finds purpose to stop.

Soul Sad

I passed an abandoned brick building today,
Highway 411 South, once a narrow
two lane open route to down
home, a super highway
now. I thought
to call
and
ask
if we ate
there when I
was a child, respite
from hot Sunday afternoons
in stopped traffic waiting on wreckers
and such, more white crosses to mark the dead.

Upon the Evening of His Passing

And the sun set in these beloved hills
we claim home. Whippoorwills called
well into the darkness. We took to our
kin and made final journeys with those
we love and name family. Within hearts
and homes, we felt the peace and warmth
of our circle and prepared to welcome
the sunrise with resolve to make the day
beautiful in the eyes of the Lord and our
family of kindred souls. Abundant peace
and love as we melt in the gloaming.

Spring Confusion

I dreamed Daddy alive a few nights ago,
    dreamed him out of order,
        dreamed him dying and gone,
           dreamed hurt again.

I dreamed Mama alive the next night,
    dreamed her out of order,
        dreamed her dying and gone,
           dreamed hurt again.

I dreamed pain,
    dreamed myself awake,
        dreamed tears,
           dreamed spirits cried.

I dreamed blue May skies marked my end,
    dreamed with eyes open,
        dreamed blue,
           dreamed clear spring.

Today

I remembered. Brother is gone.
When the mountains begin to wake,
I will miss him most. My true mountain
man. He walked trails with quiet purpose,
agility, breathed every nuance of his place,
walking stick close at his side. He covered trail
ground without breaking cadence or working sweat.

Today, I remembered.

Narrow Slit

Feeders outside this death room draw visitors.
Chickadees and cardinals scatter the offering,
selective sampling while a white-haired woman
sleeps away her pain, shuns touches and love.

Solitude gloves her old and new fears, lonely
and abandoned, tossed on the pile at hall's
end where broken bodies gather, wait under-
taker's wagon. Souls gather speed, catapult

to a quiet celebration away from dead blue
veins. She inches alone along cold corridors
of death's block house until she stops,
finds that narrow slit of fancy flight.

Steeping Home

Iron pans girded our kitchen, well-seasoned and worn,
each designated for a particular blend of ingredients,
a dash of this, a tad of that. We learned early to hold
the hard strength of cooking home. Our smallest pan
held cornbread or biscuit pone for two, used by Mama
and Daddy in a house alone, the largest round one
pulled from rest on Saturday nights. Mama and I stood
side by side, made banana pudding for Sunday family
dinner. Measuring cup, canned Pet milk, sugar, salt, eggs,
vanilla, and flour started our mix. I blended the dry with
a battered fork, stirred equal parts milk and water until
smooth. Last, medium heat, two egg yolks, beaten.
Low heat, slow stir. Vanilla last. Layers built in a Pyrex
bowl, pudding, Nabisco wafers, bananas, no meringue,
all done while we studied tomorrow. It's the steeping flavors
overnight in the Frigidaire where we honor our faithfulness.

Summer Passing

And like the wind I felt crossing my brow in dreams
of wakeful watch, Mama left. Quiet. A sharp intake.
One breath. Her head gave to one side, right hand
resting on her spaniel's back, last rock of her chair.
No sound. A long room filled with books, family
photos, both chairs alone now, memories sucked
from gatherings, caught in the fireplace chimney,
released to scatter along the drive across the creek,
lost to us all. Heat parched our throats, our lips,
our touch that July when I shut the door to home.

Spirit Place

You must be born again.
—Jim Wayne Miller,
"Brier Sermon"

Here at the spirit place, a street preacher stands, a short stout man, his weathered blue suit threadbare, shiny, his white shirt open at the neck, a wide-striped tie speckled with leftover breakfast jam and held fast mid-girth with a tarnished gold tie clasp. I've known him all my life, this street corner preacher man named Papaw Weaver, a knife trading storytelling man until Saturday morning at this corner of Market and Union, a call to preach. His open-faced black Bible drapes his left hand, his right extends to heaven, shouts for revival and for born again Christians to match his fervent pace, his one small patch of concrete, congregation Hell-bent to escape his song of sin and redemption, this scene finds its toehold. Cover my grave with this rooted inheritance. I must be born again.

Home

Now the voices changed,
somewhat less unkind,
deep in the corner.

I took a fresh hold,
started singing,
enjoying the sound.

How far I've come,
all I've tried to be
back in the mountains.

I see gray eyes,
and my eyes float
in his shining light.

Home is a long way
away, rolled up
in a quilt.

Mountain Quiet

The hard part is the waiting, that moment between the staying
and the going, when true understanding comes in and sits down
quiet beside me in the darkened room. Heart ache. We reach
across the quiet. We love the quiet, not the quiet of this moment,
but the quiet our mother raised into us before we born, the quiet

I found on the Big Frog and he found on Thunderhead Mountain,
a place he reached for today, that hard hike more than 20 miles up
over 5000 feet, when he left out of Anthony Creek Trailhead
in the Cove, took the measured steps of a man who understood
the earth. His breath and step never faltered. He gave this to me.

Quiet. Hard letting go when the staying and the going become one.

Gray Blue Days

Gray blue wraps the Appalachians
this morning, high and low,
peaks and valleys,
reminds me of Daddy's eyes,
even my own when my heart
shrouds its heart losses,
one at a time, sheds tears
like skin sloughs in spring
when temperate days
no longer need warming.

Stitched Prayers

Don't borrow trouble,
Mama warned, her own body
weighted. Years of hurt
stitched her worry like
pieced quilts her fingers
worked in prayer.

Carry Me, Love Me

Heart Breath

Fill your paper with the breathing of your heart.
—William Wordsworth

I breathe my heart onto this page. Words sanctify.
Night stars suckle the universe, our place marker.

Water tumbles along a river journey, jostles rock bed,
rounds sculpture, vibrates time, Earth's age lines.

The breathing never stops. Hearts know no end
when roots of the mighty hardwoods hold fast,
even after wind dies and souls transition.

Act IV: House to Half

Backstage, no lights illuminate my confusion.
I lose my place, try to remember if I had cues
for my next move. Stage right? Stage left?
I intuit this will make a difference in Act IV.
Time pulls me along, tugs at me to go faster.
I lag behind, curse the lack of stage directions.
Act IV requires fewer lines of dialogue. Blurred
details fail me. Thick pleated purple drapes
anticipate, offer no respite, wait to be pulled back,
wait to commence this gloaming of my life.

A Call to Love

I thought to write about love, perhaps red roses and Hallmark cards, the expensive ones, embossed, cellophane covers to protect until mailing, maybe even use a heart forever stamp, although it would take two side by side, extra weight you see, the extra weight of love, me resting against Mama's legs, my head in her lap, the brush strokes solid and sure, my hair silk and waves from her care, the extra weight of brother balancing me on his bicycle handlebars, a race home to Mama after I fell off the dugout, bottom of the seventh inning, bases loaded, brother at bat. Perhaps the shoulder weight of Daddy never knowing how to wipe our tears, tend our hearts, celebrate our walk, guide letting go. I thought to write about love, the patient kind found on our front steps, a slow walk, my knees no longer trustworthy, the last I love you at day's end, morning celebration of one more day, a call to love.

Coffee-Stained Kitchen Talk

Brewing coffee woke me every day in my child years,
a chore for the first to rise, strength dictated by the hands
dipping scoops of JFG into a two piece drip pot, never saw
its lid. It never felt soap in its belly, only scalding water
from our limestone-lined well its bath. Mama and Daddy
drank early, then kept this pot on the back burner ready
for drop-ins, Avondale coffee creamer delivered to our
front door always ready in the fridge door. Conversation
lingered hours at our kitchen table, cups grew cold. Milky
coffee coated my senses until day passed, and I cleared away
their cups and saucers. Stories stained Mama's tablecloths,
ashes from cigarettes speckled holes, settled where they sat.

June Hay Fields

He thinks to make a farmer of me, this late autumn
of our lives, tractor and tools second nature to him,
well-used limbs since he stood to drive his papaw's
Farmall Cub. Barely four years old, he worked clutch
and brakes, standing, his blonde head not quite visible
over the long-necked steering column. He proved
his worth in fields around Ellejoy, raking and baling,
even square bales a labor of joy in his sinew and bone,
like his disfigured foot crushed from the back fender
of a red tractor. Years of dust, diesel, and dirt ground
deep. Nath Brown taught him to back a hay trailer
hours after day's work done, over and over until he made
it right, and Nath said supper time, now get on home.
Stories told about the Davis fields or the Jeffries bottoms
or the Hitch place grounded our dating years and now our
porch-sitting times. After a day or two of making me a farmer,
this early June day, I pull the rake behind a red Massey tractor,
twelve acres cut and ready. He builds the first rounds and turns
me loose. We work our late day away, a row at a time.

Love Lifted

Days of memory wrap
away fear and shelter
us in layered love,
gifted from before
hearts understood.
Tears of laughter
ease our time,
rehearse,

motion of touch,
open and shelter
mined beauty today.

Papaw's Heart

Courtship began in May, long before the demands of hunting season, a bond stronger than new love, the Remington still shiny from well-used cleaning cloths, Papaw Ray in perpetual ready to load his International Scout, satisfied with just his oldest grandson, the one who became his son when daughters filled his home. Vienna sausage and nabs, a can of coke his hunter's lunch in the folds of the Cherokee National Forest. Papaw Ray spent the better part of summer sizing up this new girl, the old one not yet forgotten. He walked around the barn door in our conversations about separation and of new guns and the best way to cook venison, not sure about this hunt and new romance. Papaw Ray realized the draw of man and woman in new ground, predictable like a young buck during rut. The heart aches old when papaws watch their boys grow. He loved me, this papaw who came to me as a gift, this first hunt of new love, when his grandson and I walked Farr Gap Trail, our steps slow to meet the dawn of November heart.

Our Season of Grieving

I

This is the moment when I know the string
of breathing is tenuous. This is the last
fourth of living. I have already spent
the first three fourths on survival,
taking myself and my place too seriously—
a string cast about into both the calm
and the storm. The float bobs, sometimes
under, always coming back up.

II

It grieves me to think this could be it,
this countdown when eyes and ears,
muscles and bones, organs and blood
begin to fail us, a time of rocking
on the porch tuned into the birds.
Quiet becomes our lovemaking,
twilight comes faster, rushed, unfinished.
Tasks wane in importance, our season of grieving.

III

What will the soul do when forced out of my body?
Will it linger, hang around, flutter its wings
fast and urgent as hummingbirds at summer's
nightfall? Will the soul suck the nectar, persistent
enough to carry it beyond this porch and our rocking
chairs, beyond the moon that has found purchase on the ridge?

Scattered Remains

I wake to low clouds, thick across the ridges behind the house.
They tease rain, hide sunshine, confuse me with indecision
in today's promises. I think to finish reading four Old Testament
prophets, minor in fame, begin with Joel and Amos, randomness
in my early morning walk with scripture. My attention meanders,
climbs the rise, its highest point home to scattered remains
of a brother lost. Light heralds a premonition, perhaps Gabriel
bringing news, *The Sight* Mama called it. Visions of things to come,
like waiting on the last close kin leaving, stillness in white, confusion
around this remnant of his dying when I became the one left behind.

Whippoorwill Dream

I dreamed of whippoorwills last night calling
each other down the holler. Lovebirds woo
and mate, raise their young, start new
when babies leave the nest. Mate for life,
stay close to this side of the mountain.
Whippoorwills called back and forth
until one waited an answer that fell silent.

All the night loves cried sad.

Front Porch Haiku

1

Hummingbirds dance dawn.
Sweet water compels return,
holds their thin tongues tight.

2

Twin black bear babies
steal full feeders, mama close.
Run babies, run hide.

3

Coyotes bark close.
Ruffled turkeys fear red eyes,
circle tight nearby.

4

Cardinal shrills light.
Cowbirds bring shrouded mischief.
Sparrow hawk floats home.

5

Late evening May breeze
gathers honeysuckle sweet.
Fireflies sprinkle light.

6

Bats circle spring pond
feasting on succulent gnats
served on lawn's table.

Quilt Speak

Gentle voices laced stories in quilt castles
in my early child life, days and twilights
melted together, my head rested against
the crook of Mama's side. My obsession
with fireflies waned, my brown sweaty legs
trembled into the embrace of a glittered
sky canopy where shooting stars hid my
sweet wishes. Hate also dwells on quilt
canvases, the promises of Mama fractured
by the failures of her body. Under this canopy
of whispers I sought her crook to rest my
fears when sorrow shut the sounds of night.

Rocking Chair Porch

Slivers of broken sticks litter our front porch,
gradations of brown splinters rest against a blue-
blanketed oak glider, its measured sway controlled
by a new black puppy. Hummingbird feeders this
mid-July morning number five, strategic placement
encourages less fighting, more babies and parents
slurping sweet sugar juice. A lone turkey hen ventures
from beyond the woods line across the creek, five poults
close to her feathered skirt, breakfast bound this breaking day.
We find our rhythm with voice and silence, our seats well-worn.
Habit and time. Quiet. Back and forth. Our hearts take on this beat.

Dog Days

Words lose their way this summer.
Lines of poetry hang on the edge
of my brain, can't find their way
to the end of my pen. Images stay
hidden, refuse to join memories
like nomads looking for crystal
drinking water in parched ground.

Night of the Soul

Don't skip sweet wine,
or mountains—climb them
sideways, reach for blue
and green. Pull gardenias
gentle to your face,
rest at the church rock,
wait until dusk, plait
and unplait the last word,
leave on a single straight
track, disappear into memory.

Appalachia Old

I come from old,
> old mountains.
>> carry me, love me.

I come from old,
> old water, springs
>> rinse me, settle me.

I come from old,
> old kin, stories
>> gird me, mark me.

I come from old,
> old shape notes,
>> soothe me, promise me.

I come from old,
> old dirt patches,
>> grow me, warm me.

I come from old,
> old hardwoods,
>> brace me, root me.

I come from old.

Sue Weaver Dunlap lives deep in the Southern Appalachian Mountains near Walland, Tennessee, where she and her husband Raymond live and work a mountain farm. Here, among the bear, turkeys, deer, and pets, she writes poetry, fiction, and memoir. Her poems have appeared in *Appalachian Journal*, *Anthology of Appalachian Writers*, *Appalachian Heritage*, *Pine Mountain Sand and Gravel,* and *Southern Poetry Anthology*, among other anthologies and journals. Her poetry has won several awards. Dunlap retired from teaching in 2012 and has since taught poetry classes, done free-lance editing, and volunteered with Tennessee Mountain Writers and Mountain Heritage Literary Festival. Her chapbook entitled *The Story Tender* was released by Finishing Line Press in 2014 and her full collection entitled *Knead* in 2016 by Main Street Rag.